Workbook

for

The 5 Languages of Appreciation in the Workplace

Empowering Organizations by Encouraging People

A Guide to Gray D. Chapman and Paul E. White's Book

Gelena Reads

This workbook is intended solely for educational and personal use. It is designed to complement and enhance the original book, **The 5 Languages of Appreciation in the Workplace**, written **by Gray D. Chapman and Paul E. White.** The workbook provides exercises, activities, and additional content to aid in understanding and applying the concepts presented in the original book.

Please note that this workbook is not a substitute for the original book. It is recommended that readers use this workbook in conjunction with the original book to maximize their learning experience and comprehension of the subject matter.

TABLE OF CONTENT

HOW TO USE THIS WORKBOOK

Welcome to your interactive journey through the world of workplace appreciation and empowerment, inspired by the book "The 5 Languages of Appreciation in the Workplace" by Gary D. Chapman and Paul E. White. This workbook is designed to take your learning experience to the next level by providing you with valuable insights, actionable takeaways, and personal reflections.

Getting Started

1. Begin with the Summary: To begin, read the original book's summary. This section acts as a guidepost, providing a concise review of the important concepts, ideas, and tactics given in the book. It is your road map to what lies ahead.

2. Key Takeaways: As you go through each chapter, you'll come across "Essential Key Takeaways." These are the valuables pulled from the original book, reduced into bite-sized, actionable bits. Pay special attention to these, as they contain the main ideas of each chapter's wisdom.

3. Journal Prompts: We've included a significant tool in this workbook called "Personal Assessment Journal Prompts." After you've digested the important points

from each chapter, pause to consider how these insights apply to your own workplace experiences. These suggestions are intended to promote self-discovery and assist you in putting what you've learned into practice.

Navigating the Workbook

4. Chapter Exploration: The organization of the workbook is similar to that of the original book, with each chapter devoted to a different language of appreciation. Explore the information at your own speed, returning to themes and suggestions as needed. Feel free to scribble down your ideas, thoughts, and action plans in the margins or in a separate notebook.

5. Self-assessment Questions: As you get closer to the end of your adventure, you'll come across the "Self-assessment questions" area. You'll be able to assess your newfound knowledge and self-awareness here. These questions will help you assess your progress and identify areas where you might improve workplace appreciation.

Making the Most of Your Journey

6. Sharing and Discussion: Consider organizing a study group or discussion circle with coworkers or friends who are also on their appreciation journey. Sharing your opinions and experiences might help you gain a

better understanding and build a supportive community dedicated to workplace empowerment.

7. Practice and Application: Keep in mind that genuine transformation comes from putting what you've learned into practice. Experiment with the ideas and tactics at your workplace to see how they affect your colleagues and company.

8. Lifelong Learning: Your path does not finish here. Continue your research on workplace appreciation books, articles, and resources. This workbook is only the beginning of your continued development.

Accept this workbook as your personal guide to creating a more empowered and thankful workplace. It's more than simply a collection of pages; it's a transformational toolkit. Prepare to unleash your organization's full potential by motivating and empowering others around you.

Let's go on this thrilling adventure together!

SUMMARY

Chapter 1: Motivating by Appreciation: The Concept
This first chapter will introduce you to the core principle of inspiring and empowering yourself via gratitude. Discover how recognizing and expressing gratitude may alter workplace interactions.

Chapter 2: For Business Leaders: Understanding the Return on Investment from Appreciation and Encouragement
Study how praise and encouragement might help you as a business leader. Recognize the measurable benefits of developing an appreciation culture in your organization.

Chapter 3: Appreciation Language #1: Words of Affirmation
Explore the first language of appreciation, Words of Affirmation. Discover how real and personalized words of encouragement can enhance your workplace morale and motivation.

Chapter 4: Appreciation Language #2: Quality Time
Learn the significance of Quality Time as an appreciation language. Discover how devoting time and attention to yourself may boost your relationships with colleagues and superiors.

Chapter 5: Appreciation Language #3: Acts of Service
Explore Acts of Service as a form of appreciation. Discover how simple acts of assistance and support may have a big impact on your sense of worth at work.

Chapter 6: Appreciation Language #4: Tangible Gifts
This chapter explores the effectiveness of Tangible Gifts as a source of appreciation. Understand how thoughtful gifts can demonstrate your worth to coworkers and managers.

Chapter 7: Appreciation Language #5: Physical Touch
In appreciation, delve into the distinct language of Physical Touch. While physical touch is not always appropriate in the workplace, this chapter examines when and how it can be a powerful form of gratitude.

Chapter 8: Discover Your Primary Appreciation Language: The MBA Inventory
Using the MBA Inventory, discover your major appreciation language. Understanding your personal appreciation language is critical to earning the acknowledgment that empowers you.

Chapter 9: Your Least Valued Language of Appreciation: Your Potential Blind Spot

Recognize your least preferred language of praise to uncover your possible blind spot. Examine how this awareness can make it easier for you to handle social situations at work.

Chapter 10: The Difference between Recognition and Appreciation

Recognize the difference between recognition and gratitude at work. Recognize the benefits of true appreciation, which go beyond simple acknowledgment, and why it's crucial for your wellbeing.

Chapter 11: Motivating by Appreciation in Various Industry Sectors

Examine the ways in which the motivating by appreciation ideas hold true in various business sectors. Learn how appreciation may empower you in the context of your own workplace.

Chapter 12: The Unique Characteristics of Volunteer Settings

Learn about the special dynamics of volunteer settings and how encouragement is a key factor in keeping volunteers like you motivated.

Chapter 13: Does a Person's Language of Appreciation Change over Time?

Check to see whether your language of appreciation can evolve. Recognize how your preferences for appreciation can change as a result of personal and professional development.

Chapter 14: Motivating by Appreciation: Overcoming Your Challenges

Address any difficulties you may have receiving gratitude at work. Explore methods for overcoming challenges and promoting an appreciation-based culture.

Chapter 15: Authentic Appreciation: What to Do When You Don't Appreciate Your Team Members

Learn how to deal with circumstances where it's difficult for you to appreciate your team members. Learn strategies for establishing rapport and creating a healthy work atmosphere.

Motivating by Appreciation: The Concept

Essential Key Takeaways

1. Feeling appreciated at work is important because it helps employees recognize that their contributions are valued.

2. Employees may begin to feel like commodities if they do not feel valued by their bosses and coworkers.

3. According to Steven Covey, psychological survival, which includes feeling understood and appreciated, is a basic human need.

4. When there is a lack of appreciation, team members grow disengaged, discouraged, and may begin complaining about their work.

5. Dissatisfied personnel may consider leaving the company in pursuit of better chances.

6. A "just say thanks" strategy for expressing gratitude is frequently useless; real, individualized gratitude is necessary.

7. For appreciation to have an impact, the recipient must see it as valuable.

8. When workers don't feel acknowledged or emotionally supported by their managers, they are more prone to develop burnout.

9. Actively expressing gratitude can enhance workplace culture despite financial limitations.

10. Delivering genuine appreciation in the workplace requires an awareness of the basic and secondary languages of appreciation that people use.

Personal Assessment Journal Prompts

1. Consider a period when you experienced a lack of appreciation at work. How did it impact your performance and motivation?

_____

_____

_____

_____

_____

_____

_____

2. Consider your teammates or coworkers. How do you express gratitude to someone whose primary language of appreciation may be different from yours?

_____

_____

_____

_____

_____

_____

_____

3. Assume your boss is launching a "just say thanks" campaign at your place of employment. What effect do you believe it would have on the general spirit and drive of your team?

_____

_____

_____

_____

_____

_____

For Business Leaders: Understanding the Return on Investment from Appreciation and Encouragement

Essential Key Takeaways

1. Profitability and ROI are given top priority by business leaders, who see financial health as a crucial indicator of success.

2. A lot of executives emphasize the value of results over kind words and debate the necessity of praise in the workplace.

3. As economic conditions have changed, global rivalry and economic downturns that have an impact on staff retention have been introduced.

4. Discouragement, fatigue, maintaining a positive corporate culture, and motivating with limited financial resources are among managers' top concerns.

5. Most workers don't quit their employment in search of higher pay; instead, they frequently look for psychological benefits like feeling appreciated.

6. Employee retention and commitment are highly dependent on job satisfaction.

7. Organizations incur significant expenditures as a result of employee turnover, including hiring costs and lost productivity.

8. Managers frequently despise the resource-intensive hiring and training of new staff.

9. Verbal appreciation is rarely given to most people at work, which lowers job satisfaction.

10. Showing gratitude to coworkers can result in improved attendance, higher levels of production, and a stronger corporate culture.

Personal Assessment Journal Prompts

1. Consider your position as a corporate leader. How do you rank ROI and financial health in your company? Exist any instances where you can strike a balance between employee appreciation and these priorities?

---

2. Consider your main management worries. How can you help your team overcome problems like discouragement and fatigue without relying primarily on financial rewards?

_____

_____

_____

_____

_____

3. Take into account your employee retention strategy. How can you lower the risk of turnover by enhancing job satisfaction and fostering a culture where employees feel valued and appreciated?

_____

_____

_____

_____

_____

_____

Appreciation Language #1: Words of Affirmation

Essential Key Takeaways

1. Using words to spread positive messages to other people is known as "words of affirmation," which is a strong kind of appreciation language.

2. Highlighting accomplishments and high-caliber work with praise is an effective approach to communicate words of affirmation.

3. Verbal praise that works is specific and increases the likelihood that desired behaviors will recur.

4. Gratitude that is generalized, such as "Good job," is less powerful than gratitude that is personalized and meaningful.

5. Character affirmation is another facet of words of affirmation, praising virtues like honesty, integrity, and compassion.

6. It's important to acknowledge and praise excellent character traits in order to value an employee's inherent strengths and qualities.

7. Positive personality traits also contribute to words of affirmation by assisting people in understanding and appreciating their individual life perspectives.

8. Positive words can be said in a variety of contexts, such as private one-on-one talks, in front of others, in written notes, or in public.

9. Genuine words of encouragement are important; untrue praise may have the opposite effect.

10. It can be catastrophic to forget to vocally thank coworkers because words of affirmation have a profound effect on people who respect them as their primary language of appreciation.

Personal Assessment Journal Prompts

1. Consider a recent success at work. How would you thank a teammate who made a big contribution to this accomplishment?

_____

_____

_____

_____

_____

_____

2. Consider the admirable qualities of a coworker that you have seen. How could you express your appreciation for these qualities to them in words?

_____

_____

_____

_____

_____

_____

_____

3. Think back to the last time someone complimented you at work. How did the praise's specificity affect your performance and drive?

_____

_____

_____

_____

_____

_____

_____

Appreciation Language #2: Quality Time

Essential Key Takeaways

1. Giving someone your full attention, rather than just being close by, is what is meant by the expression of gratitude known as "quality time."

2. A typical variation of quality time is quality conversation, which emphasizes sympathetic discussion and attentive listening.

3. Listening with empathy is essential for enjoying quality time because it enables you to comprehend the ideas and feelings of the other person.

4. Making eye contact and refraining from multitasking while being listened to demonstrates sincere regard.

5. Confirm and verify someone else's feelings while also paying attention to their thoughts and the emotions that underlie them.

6. Refrain from speaking while you are listening; give them time to finish their thoughts.

7. Keep an eye out for other cues regarding their moods in their body language.

8. Even if you disagree with their conclusions, it's acceptable to express your support for them; this fosters great relationships.

9. For individuals who value quality time, shared events like team outings or activities can be significant.

10. Individuals whose major appreciation language is Quality Time need to spend quality time with coworkers and managers in a variety of contexts.

Personal Assessment Journal Prompts

1. Consider a recent chat you had with a coworker. Have you given them your undivided attention, or have you been preoccupied? How could you have more effective conversations?

_____

_____

_____

_____

_____

_____

2. Consider a common event you and your team had. How did you feel about it being appreciated? How can you make it more likely that your coworkers will have similar experiences?

_____

_____

3. Take into account your encounters with your manager. Do they spend the time necessary to hear you out and comprehend how you feel? How can you express your gratitude for their Quality Time in an effective manner?

Appreciation Language #3: Acts of Service

Essential Key Takeaways

1. Services rendered is one of the five main expressions of appreciation in the workplace.

2. When it comes to feeling valued, actions speak louder than words for people whose first language is acts of service.

3. Showing gratitude through deeds of service demonstrates your regard for and concern for the welfare of your coworkers.

4. It's important to take care of your own obligations before offering to assist others because neglecting them can have a negative impact.

5. Even if you are aware that a colleague's primary language is Acts of Service, you should always ask before assisting them. It's important to respect their preferences.

6. Volunteerism is the best way to show someone you are grateful for them; it shouldn't feel forced or forced-like.

7. Effective acts of service require that the helper have a joyful and upbeat mood at all times.

8. Modify your strategy to support your colleague's efforts and guarantee that the assignment is finished to their satisfaction.

9. It's important to finish the work you start; failing to do so may discourage rather than encourage others.

10. You may show your appreciation in the job more skillfully if you know the exact services that would mean the most to your coworkers.

Personal Assessment Journal Prompts

1. Consider a recent occasion when you supported a coworker at work. How did their attitude and the work at hand change as a result of your desire to help?

---

2. Consider an instance when you helped a coworker without first enquiring whether they needed it. What happened, and how could you have handled it differently to show your gratitude more effectively?

_____

_____

_____

_____

3. Take into account a coworker whose preferred method of expression for appreciation is through acts of service. What particular steps may you take to express your gratitude for their efforts and commitment?

_____

_____

_____

_____

_____

_____

_____

Appreciation Language #4: Tangible Gifts

Essential Key Takeaways

1. In the office, tangible gifts can send a powerful message of appreciation and support.

2. It is critical to provide the proper gift to someone who appreciates physical benefits, as the wrong gift can have little impact or even backfire.

3. It's critical to understand your coworkers' primary appreciation language, because not everyone loves actual gifts the same way.

4. Tailor your gifts to the recipient's hobbies and preferences in order to make them feel sincerely appreciated.

5. Tangible presents do not always have to be tangible goods; experiences such as event tickets or spa coupons can be equally valuable.

6. It is critical for effective appreciation to take the time to select a smart present that demonstrates that you have examined the recipient's tastes and interests.

7. Irresponsible presents presented out of habit or responsibility can miss the mark and indicate insincerity.

8. Encourage employees to communicate their appreciation language and preferences in order to build a more happy work atmosphere.

9. In some circumstances, giving the gift of time off can be a highly valued and effective approach to demonstrate appreciation.

10. Both bosses and coworkers can utilize tangible gifts to strengthen connections and foster a culture of real appreciation at work.

Personal Assessment Journal Prompts

1. Think of a time when you received a present at work. How did it make you feel, and why do you think that was the case?

_____

_____

_____

_____

_____

_____

2. Consider your coworker's hobbies and preferences. To express your gratitude, how could you select a tangible present that corresponds to what they value?

_____

_____

_____

_____

_____

_____

_____

3. Think about a situation when you wished to show your appreciation to a coworker. How can you be certain that the present you choose is thoughtful and meaningful to them?

_____

_____

_____

_____

_____

_____

Appreciation Language #5:
Physical Touch

Essential Key Takeaways

1. Because of the possibility of misinterpretation, physical touch can be a difficult language of gratitude to use in the job.

2. Initially, efforts were made to include physical touch in the Motivating by Appreciation Inventory, but this raised cultural and appropriateness issues.

3. Appropriate physical touch can indicate appreciation and support in work-related relationships, just as it is important in personal interactions.

4. Because different people react differently to physical touch, it is critical to judge how your actions are received.

5. Inappropriate physical contact can lead to problems such as sexual harassment and workplace difficulties.

6. Always obtain permission or observe colleagues' conduct to see whether physical touch is acceptable as a sign of appreciation.

7. Physical touch should be used with prudence in professional situations, taking cultural norms and individual preferences into account.

8. Keep an eye out for coworkers who have been subjected to physical abuse; they may be sensitive to any sort of physical touch.

9. Regardless of the obstacles, appropriate physical touch, such as handshakes, high fives, or back pats, can improve workplace relationships.

10. While physical touch may not be most people's preferred language of gratitude, when utilized intelligently, it may add warmth and depth to work-related encounters.

Personal Assessment Journal Prompts

1. Think about a recent workplace interaction that involved physical touch. What do you think your colleague thought of this expression of gratitude?

_____

_____

_____

_____

_____

_____

2. Have you noticed your coworkers using physical touch to convey gratitude? How might you add gratitude language into your interactions?

_____

_____

_____

_____

_____

_____

_____

3. Consider circumstances at work where physical contact is not suitable. How do you ensure that your activities are consistent with professional and cultural norms?

_____

_____

_____

_____

_____

_____

_____

Discover Your Primary Appreciation Language: The MBA Inventory

Essential Key Takeaways

1. Your primary appreciation language, like your native language, is the one that communicates the most deeply to you emotionally.

2. The four essential languages of gratitude are words of affirmation, tangible gifts, acts of service, and quality time.

3. Identifying your primary appreciation Language is critical for effective appreciation communication in the workplace.

4. The Motivating by Appreciation (MBA) Inventory is a reliable approach for determining your major and secondary languages of appreciation.

5. The MBA Inventory is made up of thirty paired statements that assist you identify your appreciation languages.

6. Understanding your major appreciation language enables managers, supervisors, and coworkers to communicate their gratitude to you more effectively.

7. The Action Checklist outlines concrete actions that correspond to your preferred appreciation language, enhancing the significance of appreciation.

8. Sharing your MBA Inventory results with colleagues might boost your work group's emotional climate and general morale.

9. Even if employees haven't completed the MBA Inventory, you can deduce their appreciation language by observing their conduct, listening to their requests, and paying attention to their concerns.

10. Effective workplace appreciation can lead to healthier relationships, improved communication, and enhanced job satisfaction.

Personal Assessment Journal Prompts

1. Think about your regular interactions at work. Can you tell which appreciation language your coworkers favor based on their actions?

---

2. Consider a recent instance in which you felt unappreciated at work. How may understanding your primary appreciation language have benefited the situation?

_____

_____

_____

_____

3. Consider discussing the Motivating by Appreciation notion with your coworkers. How could understanding each other's primary languages of appreciation assist your team dynamics?

_____

_____

_____

_____

_____

_____

_____

Your Least Valued Language of Appreciation: Your Potential Blind Spot

Essential Key Takeaways

1. Your least appreciated language of gratitude may be a blind spot in recognizing your coworkers' recognition needs.

2. Recognize that each person in the workplace may have a distinct primary language of appreciation.

3. Your least valued language of gratitude may be insignificant to you, but it may be critical to others.

4. Mismatched appreciation languages can lead to miscommunication and stress among coworkers.

5. Recognizing your colleagues' preferred modes of gratitude is critical for productive teamwork.

6. Some people value actual gifts, quality time, acts of service, or physical touch more than verbal validation.

7. Attempt to comprehend your teammates' opinions and the impact of their major appreciation languages.

8. Take the initiative to learn and speak the language of appreciation that your coworkers value, even if it is not your preferred language.

9. Make a conscious effort to plan and arrange actions that correspond to your employees' primary appreciation languages.

10. By addressing your blind spot and adapting to the preferences of your coworkers, you can ensure that everyone in the company feels valued and respected.

Personal Assessment Journal Prompts

1. Consider your least valued gratitude language. What impact might it have on your dealings with coworkers who value it differently?

_____

_____

_____

_____

_____

_____

2. Consider a recent workplace conflict caused by a mismatch of appreciation languages. How may understanding and dealing with this difference have helped?

_____

_____

_____

_____

_____

_____

_____

3. Consider a coworker whose major appreciation language differs from yours. How do you intend to speak their language and make them feel more appreciated at work?

_____

_____

_____

_____

_____

_____

The Difference between Recognition and Appreciation

Essential Key Takeaways

1. Distinguish between recognition and appreciation: Recognizing and appreciating employees are not the same thing.

2. Recognition is frequently performance-focused: Recognition is primarily concerned with accomplishments and performance.

3. Appreciation appreciates the individual: Appreciation extends beyond performance and recognizes each employee's inherent worth.

4. Appreciation is required even when someone makes a mistake: Employees should be appreciated not only for their performance, but also when they confront problems or make mistakes.

5. Recognize personal challenges: Employees may face personal challenges that affect their performance; recognition might help during these times.

6. Appreciation inspires employees to accomplish their full potential regardless of whether or not they receive rewards.

7. Recognition is limited: Half of the team is frequently overlooked, particularly those whose primary appreciation languages are Quality Time or Acts of Service.

8. Personalization is important: Not everyone enjoys receiving public acclaim; recognizing individual preferences is essential for effective appreciation.

9. Avoid fake praise: fake praise can weaken trust within an organization; real praise is required.

10. Appreciation is cost-effective: Appreciation does not always necessitate large financial investments and can be done at any organizational level.

Personal Assessment Journal Prompts

1. Think about a recent working incident in which someone made a mistake. Despite the error, how could you have showed your appreciation for their efforts?

_____

_____

_____

_____

_____

_____

_____

2. Consider your team members' preferences. How can you tailor your appreciation efforts so that everyone feels valued, even if their appreciation languages differ?

_____

_____

_____

_____

_____

_____

_____

3. Consider your organization's recognition programs. Do they appear sincere, or do they appear forced? How can you foster more real gratitude at work?

_____

_____

_____

_____

_____

_____

_____

Motivating by Appreciation in Various Industry Sectors

Essential Key Takeaways

1. Even if nonprofit employees have a strong sense of calling, they still need to feel appreciated, especially considering their frequently lower compensation.

2. Financial services employees, particularly support teams, benefit from regular encouragement in their high-pressure work environment.

3. Family-owned enterprises can have complex relationships, and family members may feel underappreciated, making appreciation vital to their success.

4. Schools, from elementary to college, encounter several obstacles, and expressing real appreciation is critical to preventing burnout among teachers and employees.

5. Medical and dental workplaces have been responsive to the Motivating by Appreciation concept, resulting in better teamwork and morale.

6. Despite their spiritual calling, church and ministry employees have a strong need for praise and support in their frequently low-paying professions.

7. By following the approach, manufacturing companies can build a healthy work culture when headed by visionary owners who understand the value of appreciation.

8. Other industries, such as law enforcement, government organizations, and hospitality management, understand the need of emotional support and praise in the workplace.

9. The demand for recognition and encouragement is universal, and the MBA Inventory has been translated into numerous languages, making healthy work environments available globally.

10. Regardless of profession or language, appreciation and encouragement are universal needs, and following the Motivating by Appreciation methodology can improve workplace dynamics in a variety of industries and cultures.

Personal Assessment Journal Prompts

1. Consider your workplace: Are there employees who may feel underappreciated, even though they have a strong sense of purpose? How can you express your gratitude to them further?

_____

_____

_____

_____

_____

_____

_____

2. Consider your function in a high-pressure work environment: How can you continually encourage your support team members to keep them motivated and satisfied with their performance?

_____

_____

_____

_____

_____

_____

_____

3. Consider your workplace dynamics: Are there family members that work alongside non-family employees? How can you successfully communicate appreciation in order to bridge any gaps in understanding and motivation?

_____

_____

_____

_____

_____

_____

The Unique Characteristics of Volunteer Settings

Essential Key Takeaways

1. In volunteer environments, people willingly give their time to help others, resulting in a sizable workforce.

2. Volunteers come from a variety of backgrounds, including students, adults, and retirees, all of whom have different objectives.

3. Contrary to popular belief, retirement does not greatly increase volunteer numbers; in fact, devoted volunteers donate more during retirement.

4. Volunteers help a wide range of organizations, such as schools, hospitals, and libraries, and their impact is enormous.

5. Volunteers not only give their time but also their unique abilities, ranging from administrative jobs to specialized vocations.

6. Volunteer retention might be difficult due to high turnover rates, but recognizing their requirements is critical.

7. Volunteers must be satisfied with their jobs because dissatisfaction leads to higher turnover and lower service quality.

8. Volunteers frequently leave because they feel unappreciated, isolated, or dissatisfied with their jobs.

9. In order to keep volunteers, organizations should emphasize social connectedness and assisting them in perceiving the influence of their labor.

10. Expressing gratitude in ways that are meaningful to individual volunteers can boost retention and effectiveness in volunteer-driven organizations.

Personal Assessment Journal Prompts

1. Consider why you decided to start volunteering. What initially drove you, and how have those motivations changed over time?

_____

_____

_____

_____

_____

_____

_____

2. Think about your present volunteer position. Are you happy with your contributions, and do you feel connected to people in your organization?

_____

_____

_____

_____

_____

_____

_____

3. Consider the significance of acknowledgment and appreciation in your volunteer experience. How could your organization show you more gratitude in order to keep you engaged?

_____

_____

_____

_____

_____

_____

Does a Person's Language of Appreciation Change over Time?

Essential Key Takeaways

1. Your primary language of appreciation, like other personality qualities, tends to remain stable throughout your life.

2. While your primary language may remain steady, various situations and life stages can momentarily modify its prominence.

3. Life stages and situations, such as family health problems, can make your secondary language of appreciation more important.

4. The precise activities that connect with your favorite language may change over time and at different stages of life.

5. Personal dynamics play a key impact in selecting which language of appreciation is most successful in a specific relationship.

6. Interpersonal factors might cause your dominant language of appreciation to shift, especially when

interacting with someone whose communication style differs from yours.

7. When a person's primary language of appreciation is adequately supplied, their secondary language may become more essential.

8. Recognizing changes in your and your colleagues' appreciation language is critical to maintaining successful communication and appreciation.

9. Regular employee evaluation meetings can help discover changes in their primary and secondary appreciation languages.

10. While your personal love languages and workplace appreciation languages may have a moderate association, they might also differ, particularly in secondary languages.

Personal Assessment Journal Prompts

1. Think about a recent difficult life event. What effect did it have on your favored language of appreciation? Did it shift temporarily in response to the situation?

_____

_____

_____

_____

_____

_____

_____

2. Consider a current coworker or supervisor with whom you have a good working connection. How have personal dynamics changed your appreciation for one another?

_____

_____

_____

_____

_____

_____

_____

3. Consider your primary appreciation language. Have you observed any shifts in its significance over time? How do these modifications effect your interactions with coworkers?

_____

_____

_____

_____

_____

_____

Motivating by Appreciation: Overcoming Your Challenges

Essential Key Takeaways

1. Overcoming obstacles to expressing gratitude is critical to fostering a pleasant work environment.

2. Because being busy is a typical barrier to appreciating colleagues, prioritize and make time for it.

3. Recognize the value of appreciation in all industries, regardless of their type.

4. Feeling burdened by present duties might make it difficult to express gratitude, but finding a balance is critical.

5. Structural and procedural obstacles may obstruct efficient communication; find logical individuals to support colleagues.

6. Understanding the benefits of expressing gratitude will help you overcome your personal uneasiness with it.

7. Recognize the "weirdness factor" while beginning to respect coworkers and accept it as a positive shift.

8. Normalize the oddness of displaying thanks at first, and use humor to ease any embarrassment.

9. Give your coworkers the benefit of the doubt and embrace their efforts to recognize you as genuine.

10. While overcoming problems may necessitate creative thinking, the effort to improve workplace appreciation is worthwhile.

Personal Assessment Journal Prompts

1. Think about a time when you were too busy to appreciate a coworker. How can you make gratitude a priority in your daily life?

_____

_____

_____

_____

_____

_____

_____

2. Consider a time when you felt awkward expressing gratitude to a coworker. What advantages may you have lost out on if you hadn't done so?

_____

_____

_____

_____

_____

_____

_____

3. Consider a structural or procedural barrier in your job that prevents gratitude communication. How can you and your colleagues collaborate to address this challenge?

_____

_____

_____

_____

_____

_____

_____

Authentic Appreciation: What to Do When You Don't Appreciate Your Team Members

Essential Key Takeaways

1. When you don't appreciate your team members, it's critical to confront the problem rather than pretending to.

2. Unrealistic expectations of team members can make it difficult to appreciate their efforts.

3. Having unrealistic expectations of yourself or others can lead to a persistent feeling of discontent and prevent true appreciation.

4. Personal irritations and disagreements might be frustrating, but they should not overwhelm the importance of recognizing strong work performance.

5. Recognize that people are unique and concentrate on whether their professional performance is satisfactory rather than their personal eccentricities.

6. A lack of clarity and understanding regarding a team member's responsibilities might lead to a lack of respect.

7. Because poor performance might be caused by external factors such as personal problems or insufficient training, it is critical to address these concerns.

8. Open, caring interactions with underperforming team members can expose the underlying causes of their difficulties.

9. Adequate training is sometimes disregarded, despite the fact that it can considerably increase job performance.

10. It is critical to have a method for regular feedback and teaching in order to build an appreciating culture in the workplace.

Personal Assessment Journal Prompts

1. Think about an instance when you had high expectations for someone else's job. Did your capacity to appreciate their efforts suffer as a result of these expectations? Explain.

_____

_____

_____

_____

_____

_____

2. Consider a team member who frustrates you because of personal differences. Despite these contrasts, how can you redirect your focus to appreciating their work?

_____

_____

_____

_____

_____

_____

_____

3. Recall a case in which you were unaware of a colleague's responsibilities. What effect did this have on your capacity to appreciate their contributions? What measures can you take to have a better understanding of their responsibilities?

_____

_____

_____

_____

_____

_____

Self-Assessment Questions

1. Think on a recent work experience in which you felt sincerely appreciated. What appreciation language was utilized, and how did it make you feel?

_____

_____

_____

_____

_____

_____

_____

2. Using the MBA Inventory, determine your dominant appreciation language. How can you communicate this choice to your coworkers or boss in order to strengthen your workplace relationships?

_____

_____

_____

_____

_____

_____

_____

3. Have you ever been in a scenario at work when you felt unappreciated or undervalued? How may grasping the difference between acknowledgment and appreciation have helped?

_____

_____

_____

_____

_____

_____

4. Think about your interactions with coworkers and team members. Are there people whose appreciation languages you find difficult to accommodate? What changes can you make to better satisfy their needs?

_____

_____

_____

_____

_____

_____

5. Investigate the concept of a "potential blind spot" in your appreciation language. What have you discovered about your least valued language of appreciation, and how can you use this knowledge to improve your professional interactions?

_____

_____

_____

_____

_____

_____

_____

6. If you are in a position of leadership, consider your leadership style. How can you use appreciation languages to more successfully engage and empower your team members?

_____

_____

_____

_____

_____

_____

_____

7. Has your dominant language of gratitude evolved over time, either personally or professionally? Consider

what may have inspired this development and how it may affect your present professional relationships.

_____

_____

_____

_____

_____

_____

_____

8. How can you use the principles of inspiring by appreciation outlined in Chapter 11 in your own industry or sector? Are there any special difficulties or opportunities to consider?

_____

_____

_____

_____

_____

_____

_____

9. How has appreciation influenced your volunteer experiences if you've been involved in volunteer settings? What techniques can you employ to increase appreciation among your volunteer groups?

_____

_____

_____

_____

_____

_____

_____

10. Consider a moment in which you found it difficult to respect your team members. What steps can you take to address these issues and create a more positive and appreciative workplace?

Made in the USA
Columbia, SC
17 November 2024

46831895R00046